contents

... a joy proposed ...

... what is your substance, of what are you made ...

... as fair

... writ in ... s strange ...

... sweet lo

... a coupl

... that wi

... what beauty is, see where it lies ...

... many a thing I sought ...

... a joy proposed ...

... then begins a journey ...

Using the very individual and in many respects unique properties of metal and metal meshes is a continuing joy for me and combining these unusual and interesting materials with a wide range of media and techniques is a journey well worth pursuing.

A fascination with 'alternative' surfaces and treatments of subjects has led me to gradually move away from traditional textile surfaces and to an exploration of anything which I could get under the sewing machine!

I began by adding glue, paint, crackle glazes, gilding and other treatments to the textile pieces which I had created, and then began to incorporate other materials into my work to construct my own surfaces.
This it seemed gave me a greater freedom of expression than any single piece of fabric could do.
Beginning with the tentative addition of embossed and burnished metal motifs onto some hangings, my use of metals gradually increased until I found myself using large sheets of copper shim as a fabric, taking time to explore and develop the relationship between metal and thread has transfigured my work completely.

I have worked with metals, gilding and patination techniques in one form or another for several years now, I continue to find that the more you play, the more possibilities are there to discover. I would urge you to play and sample ideas because once you get started you will realise that there are myriad variations in materials, scale, additions, designs and end results using these materials.

There is now a wider and more easily available selection of these media than ever before.
The medium of metal gives rise to possibilities beyond those of fabric alone, adding a completely new range of surface qualities. You can play with the sheen of the metallic surface, perhaps allowing it to be bright and catch the light, or to obscure parts of the lustre with different colouring techniques.
Using metal meshes will add a quality of strength belied by it's fine and delicate look. With the correct safety precautions, the transparency of the meshes can be exploited to allow lit structures such as sculptures, lamp shades or lanterns to be created.

I do so hope to lead you through further explorations of these unusual materials and enable you to add the medium of metal into your textile repertoire.

... and of this book, this learning mayst thou taste ...

There are a few points which I would like to make clear to you about the structure of the book. Firstly, please do take sensible precautions for your own safe use of equipment, chemicals, products and the materials, and always note safety instructions on the packaging and those which are given in '**... be of thyself so wary ...**' red boxes through the book. Other general hints and tips or snippets of use are given in '**... advis'd respects ...**' boxes and tools or equipment which you either need or will find useful are given in '**... what need'st thou ...**' boxes.

This book covers a wide variety of information. Firstly we look at the types of metal, meshes and other materials which are available to use (**... what is your substance, of what are you made...**) and the basic tools you will want to have available. In '**... as fair in knowledge as in hue ...**' we move on to the possibilities for changing the colour of the metals, including the use of chemicals, paint, embossing powders, resins etc. I have remained conscious throughout that you will need to be able to find and use the chemicals suggested. None will involve a trip to a specialist chemical retailer or need particular equipment for disposal once you have used them. You will still be able to achieve a wide range of effects with these options.

Within '**... writ in moods, and frowns, and wrinkles strange ...**' you will learn techniques and gain ideas for altering the surface of the materials.
In the section '**... sweet locked up treasure ...**' we look at non-stitched textile techniques such as braiding and weaving. These provide fascinating options for constructed surfaces and three dimensional compositions. Moving to the bit you have been waiting for, '**... a couplement of proud compare ...**', you have the chance to explore and develop increasingly more complex and interesting surfaces. You will find ideas for joining surfaces, for hand stitching and machine stitching in a variety of ways.
In '**...that with gentle work did frame ...**' we combine the previously learned techniques in the form of four step-by-step projects and then a special section '**... what beauty is, see where it lies ...**' which highlights the work of four textile workers who use metal as an important part of their repertoire.
At the very end of the book (**... many a thing I sought ...**) you will discover more information about furthering your discoveries .

by Alysn

by Bryony (age 11)

Thai Hill Tribe Headdress

Fragment of Egyptian Shawl

Detail of Thai Hill Tribe Headdress

Indonesian Headdress

... the earth can yield me ...
... as with your shadow ...
... consider everything ...
... fairing the foul ...
... confounding age's cruel knife ...

... what is your substance, of what are you made ...

materials

The following materials are offered as a guide only. They are undoubtedly not all encompassing but should be easily available and give you plenty of options for experiments and discoveries.
For textile techniques the metals which are generally available for use are **copper**, **brass**, **pewter** and **aluminium**.

> *be of thyself so many ...*
>
> The metals are generally not harmful in themselves, but it is always good practice to wash your hands after handling metals, before leaving your studio or eating etc.
> When using recycled metals make sure that they are thoroughly clean and devoid of all traces of food and drink before beginning to work with them.
>
> The edges of the metal will be sharp and when cut, the edges of the mesh can behave like small cactus spines, so watch your fingers!

As each metal does have different malleability, resilience and strength, the perfect thickness of one metal for a project will not necessarily be the same as the best thickness for a similar process in a different metal, but practice makes perfect and as you use the metals you will become much more familiar with the options and find that you have a rough scale in your head for the conversions.

You will also develop a feel for the metals properties and know whether you will find it useable for your projects.

The thickness of metals

The metals and meshes which are best used in a textile context tend to be fairly thin as for many techniques we need to be able to manipulate or to pierce a needle through the surface.

These metals are usually called 'shim' for the thicker metals or 'foil' for the very fine metals. They can be thought of as a fabric, one with resilience, malleability and structural properties not found in fabrics. The variety of metals available have differing qualities of hardness versus resilience and therefore it is worth reading about the options and perhaps trying a range of the metals before starting a project to be sure that you are working with the correct material for the job as each gives a unique finished surface for your projects.

There are at least four common definitions which are used to define the metals. These are:-

    Inches ("),
    Millimetres (mm),
    English Gauge (SWG) and
    American (Brown and Sharpe) Gauge (AWG).

The definition used will depend upon the type of metal and your supplier.

The heaviest thickness or gauge which we are easily able to work when considering textile techniques on a domestic scale is for shim metals up to 0.13 mm (0.006")(36 SWG)(0.005 AWG)
Thinner than approx. 0.06 mm (0.002")(44 SWG) (No equivalent AWG) thickness, the metals are generally considered as foils.

Full conversion charts are available in many books and on the internet if you need further details.

During this book I will give you the thickness of the metals described in both millimetres and inches.

Copper

Copper is a soft and extremely malleable metal which lends itself to all of the many colouring, shaping, stitching techniques which we will cover in this book and has an attractive warmth of sheen.
I am told that it is on a par with 24–karat gold for malleability and I know that many jewellers will practice their craft on copper before launching into the precious metals.

Copper is an elemental metal not an alloy, though I suspect that most commercial copper has trace impurities which can affect the behaviour of the metal slightly.
It is available in thicknesses from 'ultrafine' (0.012 mm, 0.0005") which behaves like baking foil, through to shims of 0.15 mm (0.005") and upwards. Any thicker than this is too tough to easily stitch either by hand or by machine, therefore you are better to consider an upper limit of 0.12 mm (0.004").

If you are given a choice of hard, half hard or soft copper which in each case comes as either cold or hot rolled, select soft, hot rolled as this is easiest to manipulate. Cold rolled copper is a harder metal with a smoother surface. It is less easy to deal with, so you will need to soften the metal before use (pg. 12).

Depending on the supplier and the metal thickness, you may be restricted to a width of 165 mm (6.5") or it may be available in up to 600 mm (24") widths. You should be able to buy the metal in either pre-packed sections or by your required lengths.

Brass

Brass is a mixture (alloy) of copper and zinc. Its' colour varies depending on the proportion of zinc in the mixture. A greater proportion of zinc will result in a more yellow colour and a more malleable metal, less will be a richer dark gold but the metal will be less flexible.

Because brass is more springy and resistant to manipulation than copper, aluminium or pewter, it is easier to work with sheets of 0.003" thickness or less. If the brass is softened or embossed then it will become more workable (see pg. 13 and 22).

Brass is generally available in widths of up to 330 mm (12") and as with the copper you should be able to buy in either pre-packed sections or in your required lengths.

Pewter

Pewter, an alloy of copper, antimony and tin is a silver with a soft hint of a light bluey-cream which is very pretty.
Though it is significantly heavier than copper, it is incredibly malleable and soft even at lower gauges (i.e. thicker!) and it does not work harden (breaking with repeated working) as other metals will. It will tear leaving enticing edges and is available in widths of up to 500 mm (20").

Aluminium

The bright silver colour of elemental aluminium is familiar to us in the very thin foil used for cooking and this on its own can be used as a material. It is a very light and malleable metal therefore very easy to use for many techniques.

Aluminium is available and usable in thicknesses from fine cooking foil to embossing metal at around 0.3 mm (0.01").

You will also find that there is available a selection of coloured and textured versions of the metal, though these are often in a thinner form than aluminium sold for use as embossing metal.
Many craft packs of coloured metal which may look like brass or copper are actually coloured aluminium.
To check whether this is what you have, look closely at the cut edge of the metal and if you see a silver layer underneath the colour your piece is most probably aluminium.

Once again the metal is available in small taster packs, A4 sheets or 300 x 900 mm (12 x36") long rolls.

Aluminium ribbon and reinforced aluminium foil can also be found which could have interesting applications.

... for ornament cloth use ...

A woven fabric made from fine metal strands can also be called a 'mesh'. This is a family of materials which can add quite different textures to the surface quality of your work or which can be used as fabrics on their own. Metal meshes can certainlybe obtained in **copper**, **brass**, **bronze** and **stainless steel**.

The usual grading for mesh depends upon the number of 'strands per inch' of the weave. There will also be variation in thickness of the strands therefore the mesh may be more or less open as a weave. For instance you may find very fine strands woven tightly gives a slippery, plastic sensation when the material is touched, the same thickness of strand woven more openly will feel like a fine chiffon.

It is fairly usual to find the woven metals split into two categories, firstly 'mesh' for the heavier grades (lower thread count) and 'woven metal fabric' for the finer material (higher thread count). In actual fact it is more useful to think of a sliding scale from a firm surface (at the 'mesh' end of the scale) to a soft, pliant fabric which looks and behaves in many ways like a soft organza or chiffon (the finest woven fabrics).
Generally the most useful ranges are from around 80 strands per inch (or 80 mesh) to 400 strands per inch (or 400 mesh). The 80 mesh is available in pieces around A2 size, the finer fabrics are available in taster pieces of any size or, like fabric, up to 1.2 m (48") wide and sold by length.

Another form of mesh-like metals are not in fact woven at all, but are lattice-cut and expanded. They are available in a range of manipulable weights. These are categorised by the size of hole in the structure, the smallest is 1/16th of an inch. Mostly available in aluminium but also occasionally in copper.

It is easily possible to find metal products which have been developed for other uses which we can adapt for use in textiles. Some of these possibilities are shown below, but there are just bound to be places you come across other metals and meshes, so keep your eyes and mind open and be willing to have a go! Think for example of the bundled and twisted coils of metal that are pan scourers or '**copper curls**' which are little twisted shreds of fine copper.

In this book I concentrate predominantly on the use of thin metal sheets and woven metals and their uses for makers who are familiar with textile techniques. Metal wires are referred to occasionally but are not considered in detail as they warrant a much larger book and deeper treatment on their own. Should you wish to know more about wires and techniques, there are many useful books to be found.

Adhesive Metals
Aluminium is available in A4 sheets with a self-adhesive backing. It is found both in a plain colour and with some fabulous etched style finishes. Its self-adhesive backing allows it to be either instantly adhered to a surface, or form part of a two sided project where other lightweight materials or papers have been attached to the sticky back of the metal. Something to think about!

Other types of self adhesive metals are found in the form of tape on rolls. Aluminium tape for car and domestic repairs is found in DIY stores, copper tape is also from DIY stores or garden centres where it is sold as 'slug resisting tape'.
My beans and hostas have not found much benefit from the tape, but it has been great for playing with in the studio!

Workers in 'Tiffany style' stained glass also use thin adhesive copper tape and so this is available from many suppliers. Other similar tapes are available in glass painting product ranges in aluminium, copper and brass colours.

Knitted Metal Surfaces
Made from fine enamelled wires in a wide range of colours, these machine knitted fabrics are found as tubes (like stockings) in various diameters. They have many uses as decorative embellishments and jewellery. They will fold, twist, layer and scrunch to form a distinctive ingredient in your repertoire.

They are made in at least two very fine wires (0.1mm and 0.2mm diameters), in a narrow or a coarse knit and in 'stockings' of different diameters.

Don't forget the great inspiration to be found from reusing or recycling materials. Many inspirational ideas for these materials can be found in the artists showcase (… **what beauty is, see where it lies** …) where artists have concentrated their creative energies upon using these materials in ways far beyond their original or intended use.

Aluminium is used in many **food containers**. Fairly sturdy foils often with a coloured coating on one side are used in this way. Tubes of **tomato** or **garlic pureé** or **pesto** etc. are also aluminium. Once they are empty, it is easy to cut off the top and bottom, slit down the side, clean and then you are left with the metal covered on one side with the manufacturers printing and on the other side, a gold-coloured plastic covering. This can be used with no further treatment or can be heated (pg. 13).

Metal foil **sweet papers** are very fine foils and are found in lovely strong colours. Nowadays I find that many sweets come with coloured cellophane wrappings around a silver-coloured foil which is not as useful. So at Easter I buy my children chocolate eggs which are wrapped in the colours of foils that I want to collect, they are happy with the treat and are well trained at saving the foil for me, a 'win-win' situation!
Soft drinks, beer, lager and cider etc. are often packaged in **metal cans** that can be used. This metal is very springy and not initially ductile, but with manipulation by embossing and/or a small amount of heating, superb results can be achieved. Think of using all of the colours printed onto the outsides of cans or by heat-treating the inner surface (which is covered in a thin plastic rather like the pureé tubes) can be interesting too.

… *be of thyself so wary* …

When cutting the drinks cans open, please take great care as the cans are thin and springy.
Wearing gloves when cutting is recommended
It is easy to be cut by the rough edges of the metal.
Wash the can first, then pierce the can near to the top and cut the top away with scissors, repeat with the bottom of the can. Cut down the side to open the can out. Trim off the jagged edges that will be around the top and bottom of the can.

by Amber (age 9)

... confounding age's cruel knife ...

One of the convenient aspects about working with these materials is that you are able to achieve many of the effects without the use of specialist equipment, so you actually need very few tools. When we talk about colouring, texturing and stitching the metals and meshes a few more will be useful but these will be identified as you need them.

... what need'st thou ...

General craft scissors
Cutting mat and **craft knife** or rotary cutter
'Thumb' or 'key ring' knife
Safety ruler
A pair of **protective gloves**
Scissors with decorative blades
Craft punches

Handling and cutting metal

For cutting straight sections of metal you should use a cutting mat under the metal, a safety ruler and a craft knife or rotary cutter as you would for cutting paper or card. For larger pieces you could use a guillotine.
You can also use scissors that have either straight or decorative blades.

... be of thyself so wary ...

When cutting areas from the metal it is inevitable that your hand will be in close proximity the blade and the sharp cut edge of the metal.

You should wear protective gloves and take care whilst cutting.

If you want to cut a shape out from within a section of metal without damaging the outer shape, perhaps because it is this outer portion that you are going to be using, I find that using a 'key ring' or 'thumb' craft blade is best as there is a better control over the stopping and starting without overcutting. Also the curves will be smoother as the blade does not slip in the way a normal craft knife tends to do.

Another option for cutting neat and repetitive shapes is to use a craft punch. When using a punch remember that if you carefully consider where you are taking the punched shapes out of the metal, you will have both positive and negative shapes to use.

... feed'st thy lights flame ...

... his gold complexion dimmed ...

...the painted banquet ...

... when heaven's sun staineth ...

... thy image should keep ...

... entitled in thy parts ...

... your sweet semblance to some other give ...

... as fair in knowledge as in hue ...

colouring techniques

... feed'st thy lights flame ...

An easy and effective way to change the colour of some metals is to burnish them with heat. Treated in this simple way allows a flowing 'heat blush' containing a wide range of colours to be achieved. This often gives inspiration for additional steps including texturing, stitching, beading or the addition of other surfaces.

You will need the equipment described in the tool box and it is important that you take notice of the information in the safety box as you must treat the equipment and the metal with respect whilst burnishing, but the effects are well worth it!

I will initially describe the results achieved by heat burnishing **copper** in different ways and with different heat sources, and then I will describe the different colours and reactions of other metals and meshes.

Four stages of heated copper

Copper heated whilst wet

... what need'st thou ...

A strong heat source such as a gas cooking hob, propane camping gas stove, plumbing torch, kitchen cooking torch or strong heat gun

Heat proof surface

Water pot large enough to plunge the metal being heated

Two pairs of pliers to hold the metal

Respirator mask when heating and materials with coatings

To heat copper, hold the metal section with pliers over the strong flame. Very quickly a wave of colour will disperse across the metal flowing out from the point of most intense heat. When the band of colour is part way across the surface of the metal, take the metal away from the heat and plunge it into the water. This will quickly cool the metal and fix the colours into the metal at that point.

You will be able to achieve different effects by leaving the metal near to the flame for different lengths of time. Your metal should move from raw copper through pinks, purples and reds to green and blues then yellow golds and eventually dark browns. The colours will vary depending on several factors including the thickness of the copper and the length of time in the heat. It may also depend on the batch of metal you are working with as some seem to change through the colours at different rates or show one range of colour more strongly. I presume that this is due to the small amounts of impurities in the metal.

When wet copper is heated, the effects of evaporation alters the heating patterns to give interesting results. For other variations, try heating the metal by moving it over the heat smoothly so that the colour is more even, or heat each edge keeping the centre away from the flame so that the colour changes only at the sides.

It is also possible to heat burnish with a strong craft heat gun or a D.I.Y. heat gun. Though the craft heat gun will take much longer than the other stronger heat sources, you will achieve a more even colour change across the metal and be able to stop this more easily at the stage you wish. To do this place the metal on a heatproof surface and heat with the heat gun until the wave of colour moves across the metal. Pick the metal up with pliers and plunge into water as before.

A point to note here is that if you touch the element of the heat gun onto the metal at any time, it will burn out the element, rendering it useless – so take care, it is an expensive mistake to make.

... be of thyself so wary ...

Ensure you protect yourself and your working area from the heat

You are using a strong heat source so do not directly touch either the source or the heated metal.

To save the temptation of touching a hot piece of metal, always hold the metal with a pair of pliers in each hand.

Always work with water next to you. This has two functions, firstly to plunge the metal into at the appropriate point during the heating process and also for your fingers in case of an accidental touch of hot metal.

If you do burn yourself take immediate and appropriate action for burns.

The adhesive copper tapes are best heated with a craft heat gun, as you are less liable to lose the stickiness of the tape.

All of these effects are more pronounced when working with larger sections of metal which you can then cut to select areas from.
Another benefit of this **annealing process** (heating and quickly cooling) copper, brass and bronze is that it will soften the metals, thus allowing us to work with slightly heavier gauges of metal than we would be able to otherwise. Try it for yourself.

If you leave the copper in a flame until you see it glowing 'cherry-red', then plunge it into the water and wipe off the soot, the metal will be duller and redder than the original providing a dramatically different surface for projects.

Any of these heat burnishing techniques can be applied either before or after texturing or embossing. Often with textured metals the colour will move across the surface at different rates as the heat source is nearer to the metal surface in some areas than others.

If you choose to heat the metal using a plumbing torch or a kitchen cooking torch, then it is best to work with the metal propped upright against a heat resistant surface and to use the gas torch with the flame pointing forward in its safest position.
Using these tools you will be able to create dots, lines and swirls of colour.

When you heat **woven metals**, use the same process as for the flat metal described above. Simply be aware that it will burnish more quickly as there is a greater surface area to make contact. The colours you will achieve are the same as those for the flat metals they are created from, but they will not be quite so distinct.

You can have fun pleating, scrunching, folding and wrapping the mesh because it is so very flexible and then apply heat from one side at a time. This can achieve patterns that look like tie-dying or 'shibori'. Continuing to heat the fine woven metals will result in holes being burned into them which gives yet more fabulous effects.

Heating the '**copper curls**' (pg. 9) is easiest with a heat gun, and by placing the curls in a non-flammable container. Beware though if you have a heat gun which blows a lot, you may find the curls scattered all over your workroom!

Copper heated to red hot and cooled

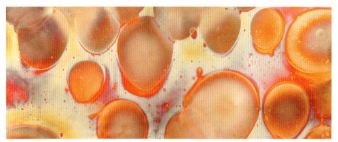
Spot heated copper shim

Heat lines on copper mesh

Copper mesh heated to four stages

Folded and heated bronze mesh

Scrunched and twisted then heated bronze mesh

Copper embossed then heat burnished

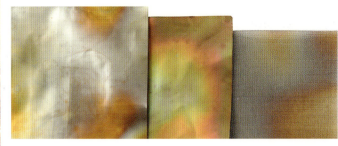

Heated brass and brass mesh

Heated stainless steel mesh

Brass shim and **mesh** shows a softer colour change than copper, giving rise to what are almost pastel tones of blues, greens, and golds.

The **stainless steel** woven fabrics will take longer to heat in order to change colour but the rewards are worth it. First appears a dull brown blush across the original steel grey, then with more heat you will achieve fantastically rich petrol blue and purple tones.

If you do decide to heat **aluminium**, ensure you read the safety notes and take great care. Aluminium (and indeed pewter) melt at a low temperature and there will be no colour change in the metal. When it is then plunged into the water the result is a finished surface of a dull grey colour which is very brittle. I know that despite me having said this, some of you will insist on trying to find an inventive way to use this trait! I look forward to seeing your results, but do take care.

Heating **reclaimed metals** gives a variety of results that can be of great interest. Puree tubes and tin cans are covered in a coating of a plastic, meaning that when placed in or near to a flame that the plastic will burn and can give rise to many colours. However, take note, the burning of this plastic will give off potentially toxic fumes.

Remember the safety instructions and only work for short periods in a well-ventilated area with a respirator facemask. Also remember that they are mostly made of aluminium therefore once the plastic covering has burnt away the aluminium will begin to melt.

Heated drinks can, pureé tube and steel mesh

... be of thyself so wary ...

Take great care if attempting to burnish aluminium or pewter as they will not change colour. They will quickly reach their melting point resulting in them dripping molten metal onto you and your working surface.

If heating drinks cans or puree tubes you should wear a respirator and work in a well-ventilated environment. You will be burning plastics that release fumes which are harmful if inhaled.

... his gold complexion dimmed ...

Changing the colour of a metal by altering its' surface chemically occurs naturally, but slowly over a period of years. You will have seen the bright turquoise green of copper on the roofs of some buildings. This verdigris is an example of a chemical change. We are able to use a range of domestic chemicals which speed up this process and can achieve a range of different colours on copper based metals.

Stainless steel, aluminium and pewter will remain largely unaffected by any of these processes. I say 'largely' rather than 'completely' because if, for instance, a stainless steel mesh is placed in the same patinating trough as copper when treated with ammonia and lime, then some of the copper oxide will transfer through solution onto the stainless steel and it will appear that the stainless steel has patinated! In all of these cases, the exposure to the air as well as the chemical is important, therefore a light covering of the chemical agent is all you need and colour will continue to develop as the metal or mesh is allowed to dry after exposure to the chemicals.

Patinas are by nature only a surface covering on the metal and liable to crumbling therefore to help to secure them, it is advisable to use a polyurethane varnish over the top.

The only equipment you will need are plastic trays to use as a trough which are large enough to place your metal and patina agents into (takeaway food trays and lids are good for small pieces).

... be of thyself so wary ...

Wear protective gloves when using proprietary patinating agents, bleach or ammonia.
Wear a face mask when using the ammonia to avoid inhaling the gas given off.

Salt

Salt gives us a very mild chemical reaction which occurs slowly and results in an encrusted, matt finish, mottled with spots of green, perhaps reminiscent of aged algae. Place metal into your trough, sprinkle over with table salt and wet with sufficient water to dampen the salt but not wash it off the top of the metal.

You will need to be patient and leave this reacting for around three weeks, keeping the salt damp throughout (a quick spritz spray daily should do it). Once you feel that there has been enough oxidation, wash off the salt and leave the metal in the open to dry. You will find that it continues to tarnish for several days.

Results of salt patination

Vinegar

Vinegar is also a mild oxidising agent acting on the metal surface and so we can treat the metal in the same way as with the salt. Lay the metal or mesh under a covering of vinegar (any type should work though I had little success with balsamic vinegar!). Leave in the vinegar for at least two weeks, or longer if you can, turning occasionally to allow both surfaces access to the air. If the vinegar dries add a little more to dampen again.

When the metal has been patinated for a while you will achieve blemished shades of rusty coppers with little dots of muted greeny turquoises.

Results of vinegar patination

Bleach

Bleach is a stronger oxidising agent and forms a really interesting powdery (sometimes encrusted and slightly raised) pistachio green verdigris on copper based metals with matt warm brown tones showing in-between.

To create this effect, cover your sample in sawdust (if you don't have any in the garage, some animal beddings are sawdust) then pour household bleach onto the sawdust and leave it in the trough. As with the other treatments it is best to keep the metal damp to encourage the reaction to occur. You can leave shim metal in the trough for several days but mesh, fine foil and ultrafine foil should be left only for one or two days as it will then rot away to nothing which would be a shame!

Results of bleach patination

Results of ammonia patination

Results with patina agents

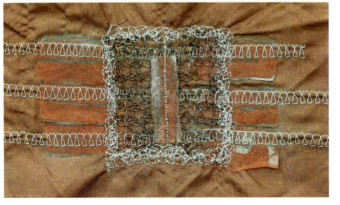

Ammonia

This patination technique creates a bold and rich lapis lazuli or sea blue finish. It often etches deeply into the metal surface producing a lava-like disintegrating surface. You must take note of the information from the main 'Safety Box' (pg. 15) and probably work outdoors, storing the covered tray out of the way of your normal life as it does rather stink!

You will need household ammonia cleaning fluid, this is usually found as something like a 10% solution and is available from chemists, and lime based (Fullers Earth) cat litter both of which can be purchased from your normal grocery stores.

Begin by covering your metal samples with the lime based cat litter and then pour ammonia solution over the top. The greater the amount of ammonia - the quicker the reaction will occur. However, so long as the litter is damp with ammonia solution then you will see an amount of reaction.

Ammonia is a powerful chemical agent and reacts strongly, so mesh and fine metal foils will disintegrate very quickly. You can experiment with the process, but depending on the amount of ammonia you have added, the reaction might only take a few minutes. You will only need to leave the fine mesh and foils in contact with the solution for a few hours or for a day at most. With shim copper, brass and bronze then any length of time up to a week should be fine.

Proprietary patinating agents

There are a variety of proprietary agents available (those bought from art materials suppliers). I use the 'Metal Effects®' Patina Solutions' which will react not only with the 'Metal Effects®' Reactive Metal Paints, but with metals or metal based substances. There are four solutions to mention, each of which will produce a different colour of patina when dry. These are: Blue, Green, Black and Rust (The 'rust' solution will give the same colour as 'green' on the metals which we are using and a rust colour if applied to iron objects.)

To use these agents, place your metal into the trough and pour the patina solution over the top to cover. The solution tends to form globules on metal surfaces and will settle into any creases or hollows on the metal surface, leaving very distinct sections of patination. The solutions do react quickly and strongly and are quite corrosive on the meshes and fine foils so only leave these in contact with the solution for a few minutes before checking them. Otherwise you can leave shims in the tray until the patina solution has dried through evaporation. The effect on metal mesh is often a smoky layering of colour.

Great results are achieved by embossing the metal first or folding or scrunching the mesh (pg. 22-23) so that only some areas are in contact with the oxidizing agents which you choose to use.

Remember that all of these agents, especially proprietary brands, bleach and ammonia will all weaken the metals because they are eating into the surfaces of what are already thin shims, foils and meshes and this should be taken note of when planning your work.

If you choose to make a piece of embroidery containing metal or meshes and then to use a patinating agent over the whole piece, you will find that most threads will change to a green colour or indeed may rot away with the strong chemial agents. In these cases use man-made threads - this includes the option of nylon invisible thread.

...the painted banquet ...

Rub

Many water-based paints are not suitable for colouring metal as they are not able to adhere onto the metal surface due to its' smooth and non-absorbent surface. Though **acrylic paints** do not form a completely secure connection to the metal, if the surface is first cleaned from grease and sandpapered or rubbed lightly with wire wool, we can achieve a reasonable attachment. I find that acrylic paints are suitable for use with metal when used in the ways described and have more than enough adhesion and resilience to be stitched into successfully.

First, paint a layer of acrylic paint over the metal, leave for a minute or two to become a little sticky, then rub most of this paint off again with your cloth or paper towel. This first layer of paint adds a delicate glaze over the metal surface and as you continue to add layers of colour (three or four being sufficient) a more interesting surface will be achieved which still allows the glow of the metal surface underneath to show through.

If the metal has been textured first by embossing (pg. 22) and painted with acrylic, then remove some of the top surface with wire wool or sand paper, you will highlight the patterns embossed into them.

Taking your thoughts on a little further, why not drip alcohol based inks over this to create a transparent glaze of another colour over the acrylic?!

Scratch

Because the paint's adhesion to the metal surface is not complete, if you take a texturing or embossing tool and scratch into the paint surface you can remove the paint in areas, creating sgraffito effects.

Print

Paint can be applied by print roller directly onto metal shims or meshes. These do not have to be flat to start with, try scrunching, pleating or folding the mesh so that the paint does not catch all of its' surface. Try embossing the metal first or place a masked shape (stencil) onto the metal or mesh before rollering paint over the surface. Build upon these effects by layering this with other masks and paint layers.

Acrylic paint or other printing media can be used with printing blocks in the same way that you would print onto any other surface. Load your print roller with paint, run it across your print plate and then press the plate face down onto the metal or mesh, supported underneath with a pliant printing pad and press firmly all over (or use a clean roller to press down evenly). Carefully pull the print plate away from the metal and leave the print to dry.

Another of my favourite printing methods is to make a mono-print plate. To do this, load paint onto a roller and roll this paint off onto a flat acrylic plate - the paint should be even and not too thick. Then draw into this paint surface with something such as a wooden stick or an embossing tool, or press a textured object such as a scrunched rag or a print block into the surface which will remove paint from some areas. When you are happy with the results, use this plate to print your metal as before. Do wash your surfaces and tools soon after use when working with acrylic paints as they quickly dry and will then not be easy to clean.

what you'll need ...

- **Brushes** (cheap flat brushes are fine)
- **Dry cloth** or strong tissue
- **Print rollers**
- **Printing pad** (this could be newspaper or layers of fabric)
- **Printing blocks** (try wooden print blocks, rubber stamping blocks and mats, or create your own designer prints using materials such as PZCut mats, heat'n'form blocks, Pressprint or food tray blocks you have created yourself etc.)
- Acrylic or glass **printing plate**
- **Fine sandpaper**

Layers and rubbing

Embossed, painted and sanded

Scratched surfaces

Printed metal meshes

17

Spread

You can add textures or patterns to your pieces by adding texture gels randomly onto a metal surface, or by pressing a print block into the gel applied on the metal, or by using the gel as a printing medium on a print block. Texture gels can be mixed with acrylic paint before use or paint can be applied after the gel is dry. The gels adhere better to woven metals than to foil or shim.

Gesso

Gesso adds a flexible covering over the metal or mesh with a much more permanent adhesion than paints. It will completely cover the surface of the metal with a matt, usually white, finish. Coloured gessoes are available or you can mix pigment into the gesso before using it, and you could stitch or glue other materials to your metal or mesh before applying the gesso.

Despite hiding the nature of the metal that you have used, this method will provide a surface which has the qualities of stiffness and manipulability of metal.

Adding colour over the gesso is easy and effective.

You can add any paint or pigment over the surface of the gesso, including materials which would not adhere to the metal on its own – such as dyes, silk paints, decorators chalks, alcohol inks etc.

If your metal has been embossed first (pg. 22) sanding with fine sandpaper or wire wool will allow some of the metal to show through. This is less successful with mesh as the gesso gets into the weave and doesn't want to leave.

Because of its' flexibility and good adhesion to the metal, gessoed metal surfaces are no problem to stitch into.

... when heaven's sun staineth ...

Alcohol Based Inks

Using alcohol inks gives a transparent glaze of colour on the metal surface. These do not affect the metal's properties at all as they are a very fine coating of colour, and have the distinctive property of allowing the sheen of the metallic surface to be unaffected, though they do not necessarily form a water resistant surface on metal.

The inks are very easy to use. You can simply drop the inks from the bottle onto your samples or spread or dab them onto the metal's surface with a cotton pad and allow it to dry. The inks dry extremely quickly. If you add further layers of ink onto the surface, you will find that the reaction is very different to that of water-based paints because the inks will merge into each other and move on the metal surface again.

If the inks are wiped across the surface of a previously embossed metal, then just before the inks are dry this is rubbed with a cloth, the colour of the inks will remain in the ditches of the embossed pattern but be removed from the top surfaces.

The colours achieved when inks are applied to metal mesh are less bright, however they still provide an effective and quick colouring method.

If you wait until after stitching the metal onto a background, you can also use the inks to stain the background blending the colours across the different surfaces.

Dripping or sponging ink onto copper curls and pan-scrubbers looks great!

Texture gel prints

Gesso combined with other colouring methods

Alcohol Inks

It is possible to combine alcohol ink, permanent stamping ink and embossing powders (see below) in creative ways which leave the reflective qualities of the metals to show through. Especially effective for this purpose are the clear powders as you can apply the inks onto the metal before adding these, or interesting effects can be achieved by adding the inks onto a heated and melted powder coated surface. These surfaces are a little brittle for stitching into however holes could be pierced into the metal before the enamelling or enamelling be applied after stitching.

Mixing embossing enamels and alcohol inks (samples by Pat Shearing)

Also look out for permanent ink pads and pens which will act as resists when heat burnishing.

Nail Varnish, glass paint and ceramic paint
Glass paints and nail varnish create translucent, permanent coloured surfaces to your materials, ceramic paints are opaque.
Nail varnishes are found in all sorts of colours from bright to very pale, often pearlised or containing glitter, some are ultraviolet reactive or 'glow in the dark' which could be fantastic fun!
Glass paints tend to be made in strong, bold colours; ceramic paints are often more muted tones. Look out for both solvent based versions (which are air drying but remember that these need the correct solvent for cleaning your brushes) and the waterbased ones which require heating to set onto a surface.
These paints remain a little flexible when dry and apart from cheap nail varnishes, will not break off when stitched into.

Glass paints and nail varnish

... thy image should keep ...

Embossing powders are a very popular and versatile medium for many art and craft practices, they are fine powders available in many colours which melt and adhere to surfaces with heat from a craft gun.
The three main forms which I use are:

> **Embossing powders** will cover the entire area usually with a metallic or a gloss finish;
> **Ultra-thick embossing enamels** (UTEE) give a thicker denser surface or can be melted rather like wax and poured over surfaces, particularly useful are the clear, interference and pearl powders;
> **Distress embossing powders** cover the surface with a matt finish and crumble away to give a worn and aged effect. The colours in these powders tend to be muted and subtle.

... what need'st thou ...

Craft heat gun
Heatproof surface
'Tidy Tray' or similar to catch embossing powders
Soft brush to brush powders back into their pot

You need to first create a wet, glued or sticky surface by using a stamping ink or glue pad in random shapes or in patterns by using a print block of some sort. Sprinkle the embossing powders over this and remove any unwanted powder gently with a dry flat brush.
I find it most efficient to work into a 'Tidy Tray' so that the excess powder can be rescued and reused.
Then place your work over a heatproof surface and melt the powder with a craft heat gun.
Once the powders have been attached to the surface, they will stay put, and the metal or mesh can be further heated or patinated and the embossing powders will be unaffected , indeed they can form interesting resists.
You could continue to experiment with other heat reactive media such as FuseFX (pg. 30) or puff paints.

Embossing powders, FuseFX and Xpandaprint

Embossing powders and heat burnish

... entitled in thy parts ...

Epoxy resins are used by many jewellers and I find that they can be used simply and effectively in many ways, adding another sort of colour and finish which can resemble enamel finishes. The technique is most effective onto textured or embossed metal.

Use a two part clear resin mix (such as Araldite®), squeeze a small amount onto a piece of baking parchment or similar (it will have to be thrown away afterwards so nothing precious!) and mix them together. Once mixed the resin should be scraped with a flat tool such as a glue spreader onto the embossed metal, wiping into the dips and off the tops of the metal as far as possible.

Try these three suggestions for ways of colouring the clear resin:

You can mix in small particulate items such as glitter, pigment powders, mica flakes etc. to the resin mix and these will be embedded into the resin when it sets.

Or sprinkle powdered pigment (artists, PearlEX etc.) or metal powders over wet resin once the resin is spread on the metal and allow to set. A little powder will rub off but most will adhere to the surface of the resin, this gives a powdery metallic effect.

Or drip alcohol inks into the wet resin when on the metal to give a lovely transparent finish.

The thinner areas of resin can still be stitched into after drying, but the thicker areas can either break your needle (hand or machine) or chip off. Therefore keep your stitching to around the edge or apply the resin over the metal once it has been stitched.

... your sweet semblance to some other give ...

It is possible with some of the **transfer papers** and **paints** to apply colour to metals and meshes. There are many varieties and brands to try. With these you are able to transfer detailed patterns or images onto the metal surface.

When using transfer paints or disperse dyes, use a good strength of colour as the reflective surface of metal tends to interfere with the colour and pattern you apply.

Other transfer media are printable transfer papers and waterslide decals such as Lazertran®. These allow you to transfer images from your computer, via a special paper onto surfaces including metal. To acheive a good image is a little tricky and you may need to practice, one tip is to use spray mount on the metal and printed paper before ironing and soaking off the paper backing!

Also available is InkAID™ with which you coat any substrate, such as metal. The substrate is then primed to receive images by feeding the substrate through your printer.

... what need'st thou ...

Small pieces of **non-stick paper** for mixing glues
Glue spreader and **cocktail sticks** or similar to mix resin and powders
Protective gloves if you wish
Dust mask if you are using fine powders

Epoxy resins with a mix of colouring techniques

... be of thyself so wary ...

Resins give off fumes whilst the two parts of the mixture are reacting and fine powders such as bronze powders can be harmful to respiratory tracts so please note any safety instructions on the packaging and wear a face mask whilst working with these media.

Transfer print on aluminium

... be of thyself so wary ...

Some of these media need heat from an iron to transfer the colour which means that the metal gets hot, please take care when handling the metal immediately afterwards.

It is important that you read and follow the manufacturers' instructions for all of these transfer methods, especially when putting unusual substrates through printers.

… writ in moods, and frowns, and wrinkles strange …

patterning and texturing

... dig deep trenches ...

Altering the surface texture and qualities of metals allows you to create either defined patterns or more random forms this will then reflect light from metallic surfaces in complex ways and introduce areas of design to complement your piece.

First drawn lines on a thick embossing mat

Deepening embossed areas

Outlining embossed areas on a firm surface

Using a wipeout tool

To begin embossing, place your flat metal onto a soft or medium surface. Take an embossing tool from those suggested in the tool box and press down to draw onto the metal. This will push the marks you make into the metal. Experiment with straight lines, cross hatching, stabbing marks, swirls and spirals etc.

If you have a particular pattern in mind, place a piece of paper pre-drawn with your design on it over the metal and emboss through the paper onto the metal.

To make deeper marks after this initial stage, flip the metal over on a soft mat, and using a wider embossing tool push into the metal, stretching it into deeper grooves.

The edges of patterns can be redefined using either a silicone finishing tool or the original embossing tool by placing the metal onto your hard embossing surface and drawing around the outlines of the design.

One of the joys of using these soft metal shims is that if you wish to change an area of embossing, you can take a flat silicone wipeout tool and pull it hard across the metal surface to re-flatten it. Note however that this does not completely remove the pattern from deeply embossed surfaces.

Another effective method to texture metal is to place the metal (shim or mesh) on a piece of soluble film (this is to protect the machine bed and make stitching easier) then run the metal around under the needle of the machine with no thread in the machine. This gives a pierced surface.

Try also taking a piece of metal and placing it over any other firmly textured surface such as a stone or a tarmac surface then, using a paper stump tool and a firmer embossing tool in turn, rub over the metal until the pattern underneath has been highlighted and is impressed into the metal surface. This is the same technique required to take impressions from hard plastic embossing plates or wooden print blocks, both of which are found in many sizes and designs.

Embossing and texturing

Once the metals have been embossed or textured, many of the colouring techniques described can be used to great effect including heat burnishing, patination, acrylic painting, gessoing and alcohol inks.

Worked over embossing plates

If you need to create very deep patterns and do not want them to be flattened by later manipulations then you should fill the indentations from behind with 'plaster of paris', household filler or resin to support the patterns.

... beated and chopped ...

The woven metals and the ultrafine foils do not hold embossed patterns well, however they do lend themselves very well to the creation of a wide range of textures by folding, twisting, scrunching, pleating, plaiting etc.

Textures of woven metals

Embossed copper and stitched silk papers, coloured with patinating agents and highlighted with gilt wax

... sweet locked up treasure ...

weave, beads and braids

... a two fold truth ...
... what good turns ...
... golden tresses ...

There are many textile techniques that do not involve stitch;
weaving, braiding and bead-making being exciting options for experimentation.

... a two fold truth ...

The fundamental principles of weaving are easy to understand whilst it is also eminently possible to develop new perspectives into the technique with these materials.
You could choose to work very small, using the pieces as jewellery or hair pieces; or a little larger for book covers and wall panels; or at the opposite extreme, you might explore working on a very large scale to create hangings or art quilts! Your weaving can be extended by attaching it onto a textile panel.

To begin weaving take a piece of metal and cut to a size a little longer and wider than you wish the finished piece to be. (This allows for ease of handling and for finishing techniques.)
Cut this into strips leaving a small section at the top edge un-cut thus creating a fringe. This will form the 'warp' of the weaving and could be cut in neat or wavy lines, in equal or unequal proportions
Use tape to secure the top edge of the fringe onto your work surface.

Make a selection of 'weft' strips, the simplest weft is a strip of metal or mesh approx. 25 mm (1") longer than the width of the main piece.

Lift every other warp on your metal fringe and place a weft along the gap, drop back over all of the lifted warps. Lift the opposing set of warps (those which were down previously) and place another weft into the gap, then drop these warps and continue until you get to around 10 mm (1/2") from the bottom of the warp.
To weave in this most conventional manner, the rule is 'under – over', in other words the weft passes under one warp, over the next, under the next and so on for one row, then on the next row, the weft passes under the warp which it has passed over on the previous row. You could decide to ignore this pattern and weave randomly or in odd patterns .

The simplest finishing method is to fold every other metal warp around the back of the final weft and then to tuck any metal or mesh edges away under the weaving, giving them a little squeeze with pliers to firm up the fold.
Remove the tape to release the weaving from the work surface.

When weaving consider including contrasting surface types and textures, for instance, mixing different types of materials as wefts. Colouring, pleating, plaiting, twisting or scrunching the metal or mesh or embossing the metal or wrapping it with wires. Adding wires (beading wire, craft wires or reclaimed electrical or telephone wires) and beads as additions are all ways to extend the basic principles.

Weaving in progress

... what good turns ...

Bead making is easy and fun and can be developed according to your desires.

Using the same fundamental principles used for making decorative paper beads, you will need to cut sections of metal shim or mesh in shapes as suggested in the picture. Generally these are long thin rectangles or long triangles (equilateral or right angled). Take an end of your metal shape and wrap it around itself using a straight, smooth object such as a large needle or a knitting needle to wrap it around. Add a small touch of strong glue such as contact adhesive under the last section of the metal, allow this to dry and then remove the bead from the shank. Simple!

The fun bit is deciding what surface colouring or patterning you want to add either before or after the bead is rolled – think about texturing, patinating, painting, adding other surfaces to the bead and so on. These beads make great statements when used to embellish embroideries or weavings, for adding into tassels and fringes from hangings, or as jewellery on their own.

Beads, beads, beads ...

... golden tresses ...

Braiding gives a securely edged, flexible, decorative strip which can be a finished object in its own right or which can be further embellished and attached to other surfaces.

A basic braid which most people know is a plait. To plait, three long sections of metal are folded over each other in turn and in this order: outside right over the middle, outside left over the middle, new outside right over the middle and new outside left over the middle etc. until complete.

Simple braids

The process of braiding is similar to plaiting though you start with more than three strands.
It does not matter whether you use an even number of strands in each side of the braid or an odd one, or choose to use differing numbers of strands for each strip of the braid. By varying these options you create different patterns in the braid. A more creative outcome is achieved if you use at least two different materials or surface finishes for your strands. Explore different widths of strand; strands which are cut into wavy lines instead of straight; textured surfaces such as embossed metals or scrunched and twisted meshes; metal which is a different colour on each side and so on.

Pic. 1

The width of the braid created is dependant upon the width of your starting strips. For instance, two strips of 30 mm (1 1/4") will give a braid approx. 45mm (1 3/4") wide. Think of trigonometry if you want to work this out, or cheat, by drawing the widths of your starting strip at 90 degrees to each other and measuring the distance along the hypotenuse of the triangle formed. Alternatively, just make your braid and see how wide it becomes!

Pic. 2

The length of braid you will create, given any starting length of metal strip, will vary depending upon both the number and the width of the strands, but will be less than half of the length of your original strips.
For a basic braid (which is somewhat akin to weaving but worked on the diagonal), begin by cutting two long **strips** of metal into thin **strands**, leaving one end of each strip joined together as a fringe.
Attach these onto your work surface with tape in the shape of an arrowhead pointing away from you and so that one stip lays over the other. Fold both strips away from you to begin (Pic. 1).

Pic. 3

Fold towards you every other strand of the righthand strip, then lay one strand ('**a**') from the lefthand strip over these. Fold strand '**a**' downwards to form a new strand, laying it parallel to the righthand strips (Pic. 2).

Swap the strands on the righthand strip 'up for down' and 'down for up'. Lay the second strand ('**b**') from the left across these and fold down strand '**b**' as you did strand '**a**' (Pic. 3).

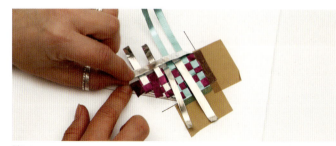

Pic. 4

Continue until you have braided all of the lefthand strands across for a first time.
The next strand to braid will be the one furthest on the left. This was also the first of the strands from your righthand strip. Fold this and lay it across all of the other strands on the row (Pic. 4).

By now the pattern and rhythm of the braid will be emerging for you and make the pattern easier to understand.

Continue working like this until you run out of free strands (Pic. 5).

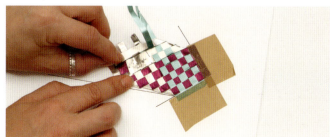

Pic. 5

There are of course many different and exciting styles of braid and various construction techniques from all around the world which you could investigate further, adapting them for use with metal shims and meshes.

... a complement of proud compare ...

...for how do I hold thee ...
... so all my best is dressing ...
... but figures of delight ...
... are vanishing, or vanished out of sight ...

Here we address practical issues which you need to consider for stitching with metal shims and woven metals and the possibilities for combining surfaces.

As with any creative activity, the use of one medium should not be seen as separate or exclusive.

The potential for combining disparate surfaces is an exciting prospect. Consider the attraction of the manipulations and changes which we have covered with the metals alone , then add to this other media, fabrics and surfaces which are already in your personal repertoire, add to this other explorations to come and you begin to conceive that the world of art and textiles has again become a wider playground.

Imagine the sheen and reflectivity of metal juxtaposing the richness of plush velvets, leather or treated papers; the fragility of aged and antiqued metallic surfaces; the smooth resistant surface of metal alongside pliant or web-like fabrics and meshes of thread …

Let's not forget also that the process of stitching directly into a metal is a physically satisfying process!

…for how do I hold thee …

Many of the joining techniques which would be relevant for other metal craft workers such as soldering or contact adhesives are not particularly suitable for combining with fabrics and threads either because they require heat, which is not practical with delicate , or because the method creates a solid surface which would be difficult to stitch through.

An alternative is **transfer adhesive** which is activated by heat. This is sufficiently strong to hold the very fine foils such as ultrafine copper or metal sweet papers.

In these cases the transfer adhesive can be placed directly between a layer of fabric and the foil. Use baking parchment over the foil to prevent the iron sticking to any stray adhesive and iron to activate the adhesive.

An alternative treatment is to iron foils onto the transfer adhesive as one piece then to cut shapes from this, rearrange these onto a backing fabric and iron down. Or foils could be ripped into small pieces and placed randomly down on a transfer adhesive backing, ironed, then cut and reapplied onto a background.

As the foils are so fine you are able to easily work into them after bonding.

These techniques will all produce interesting backgrounds ready for embellishment, this could be with embossing powders, Appliglue or puff paint with transfer foils applied over them, leading into stitch and beads or accent beads etc.

The ultrafine copper looks especially rich when placed on a velvet or an Angelina background and can be securely bonded prior to stitching.

Bonded with transfer adhesive and printed with embossing powders

Bonded with FuseFX, puff paint, transfer foils and accent beads added

Ultrafine copper bonded to Angelina fabric

Bonded and stitched sweet paper foil

FuseFX bonding

FuseFX

A relatively new medium for attaching surfaces together which can be used in interesting ways is called 'FuseFX'. It is a heat activated glue similar to transfer adhesive that comes as fine web in white or black.

(I keep finding new things to use this material for, so get your experimental head on and see where it takes you!)

In many ways the FuseFX can be used in the same ways as transfer adhesive. You will need to take the same precaution of using baking parchment both under and over the pieces you are ironing to protect the work surface and the iron.

If black Fuse FX is ironed directly to a background, including the metals with which we are concerned here, you will find that you have a decorative web-like background. You can also use FuseFX to stick foils and shims together in layers, or layer Fuse FX over the top of a surface to add another effect.

It can also be used in conjunction with embossing powders and transfer foils.

If lightweight items are wrapped in a cocoon of FuseFX and heated with a heat gun they will form a loose three dimensional textured mass. This can be enhanced with embossing powders sprinkled on, these should be added whilst the FuseFX is hot and then quickly reheated with the heat gun.

Angelina® fusible fibres

Though not perhaps the most obvious combination, I really love the effect of adding an Angelina® fibre surface over metal. It creates a shimmering, iridescent surface.

Place a small amount of 'Hot Fix' Angelina® fibre into a sandwich of baking parchment and iron the fibres on silk setting until they are fused. Take the fused sheet from under the parchment, take hold of one end of the fused Angelina® and place the iron down onto the other (taking care not to get to close to your hand). Don't press down too hard and pull the iron and the hand holding the Angelina away from each other.

The Angelina® fibres will begin to soften so that as the iron moves along the fibres, the fibres stretch. The fibres will, surprisingly, not stick to the iron! It may take a few attempts to understand this action, but soon you will feel the softening and dragging of the fibres.

Adhere the Angelina® pieces to the metal with transfer adhesive.

The Angelina® will be lightly, but sufficiently, adhered to the metal to allow you to stitch and complete the surface.

Dragging the Angelina® fabric

Bonding Angelina® to metal

... so all my best is dressing ...

Setting up for hand stitch

To begin **hand stitching** into metal, I use a flat embroidery frame with silk pins, as to force metal or mesh into a traditional hoop type frame will bend and distort your metal. It is very difficult to re-flatten the metal once it has been crushed. Whether you want to use a frame or not depends on the backing fabric, the design and sometimes at what stage in the process you are at. For instance, I find it easier to attach the metal to the backing fabric without a frame, holding the piece in my hand to get a good grip on the metal. Once the elements are attached, then a frame is useful to hold the piece steady.

A needle with a sharp point and reasonably sturdy will be suitable.

Hand stitching metals and meshes can be quite wearing on the hands and a thimble will prevent sore fingers. Most threads are acceptable for use, though the machine embroidery rayons and the metallic or glitter threads are much more likely to shred. In these cases, use short lengths of thread and put up with re-threading the needle regularly.

Textured metal threads couched into patterns

Creating a series of 'threads' using crumpled, twisted, pleated and plaited metals and meshes will give a fantastic array of ideas for couching, as will embossed and coloured metal with clustered beads and hand stitch.

Beads and hand stitch

It is difficult to pierce the surface of epoxy resin and some of the UTEE powder techniques (pg. 19- 20). In these cases, I ensure that I have an area or areas in the design which have a very light cover of resin or powder to enable easy stitching.

At the opposite end of the scale, hand stitching into the foils causes them to tear and crumble, making it difficult to hand stitch, so secure the foils with transfer adhesive first and work with a fine needle. This will lessen the amount of tear, though not eliminate it. Try to accept this disintegration of the surface and make it a creative part of your work!

... advise'd respects ...

Beware – where you place sewing pins as metals and meshes retain pin marks as holes, so you will need to think where these marks are acceptable or can be hidden without detriment to the piece.

... but figures of delight ...

When you begin to consider **using your sewing machine** to work into metals there are a few general tips to get you started.

Which threads to use? A plain sewing thread is best as it is stronger and will not shred so much as more delicate threads. I reserve the use of these specialist threads for light meshes or to embellish once the first layer of stitching is complete.

Which needle to use? Contrary to popular expectation there is rarely a problem with machining into metal. A standard 90/14 needle is fine. The finer needles will begin to break on the metals, much heavier and you will begin to punch such large holes that you will see only the hole and not the thread.

How to secure the metal? The metals do have a nasty habit of moving as you stitch and ending up in a very different orientation to the one you wanted them in! (The mesh and the knitted fabrics are not such a problem), so it is important to ensure that the pieces are where you want them.

With a little care you can pin the metals and meshes into place before stitching, but they will 'pin mark' very obviously and so the pins should be placed in strategic or discrete places.

I prefer to hold the pieces into place by hand and to get a quick securing outline of stitch before the detailed and decorative stitching.

Which fabrics work well with metals? You can use any fabric or other media you wish. Fabrics with a pile such as velvet and felt are especially good, but also silks, leather, suede, denim, fibre papers, treated papers, Angelina® and so on, are all fantastic surfaces to work with.

... advise'd respects ...

As you machine stitch, the needle punctures the metal forming a tiny crown of sharp points on the underside. As you continue to stitch, these tiny crowns scour the bed of the machine causing scratches as the work is moved around.

In order to prevent this as much as possible, it is best to stitch into metal with a backing of some kind, this might be a plain fabric, a stabiliser or soluble film.

Stitching with the feed dogs up

You do not have to use free machine embroidery to stitch these materials. By using straight, zigzag and automatic pattern stitch settings you can achieve many interesting results.

If you are able to reduce the foot pressure on your machine, then do this as it will help to prevent the metal being pushed out of place as you stitch and may stop the foot marking the metals at the side of your stitching.

In order to help you learn and to get a feel for stitching into metal on your machine, I suggest that you try at least some of the following exercises, each of which creates a different type effect of which you might want to use later.

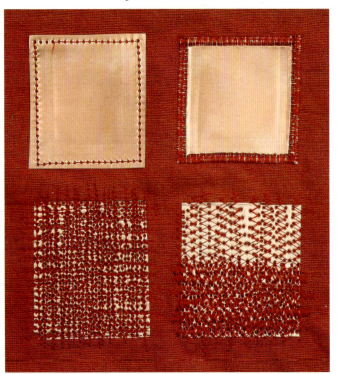

Stitch exercises

• Place a small piece of metal onto a backing fabric and place a stabiliser under this. Then stitch around the metals' edge with a long straight stitch.

• Repeat the above exercise, and after this set your machine to a zigzag which is wide enough to cover both the straight stitch and go over onto the backing fabric. Set the stitch length to be as short as you can to create a satin stitch. Work right around the edge of your metal. This gives a very bold and blocked edge. But remember, the first straight stitch will have held the metal piece in place. You may be in danger, if your machine does a very close satin stitch, of perforating the metal so much that it cuts the piece out from the centre, watch for this!

As an extra excercise here, you can set your machine to an automatic pattern and stitch around another piece of metal.

• We are also able to alter the appearance of the metal surface very dramatically by covering the metal and some of the background with lots of close stitching. Try running across a patch of metal several times and in more than one direction with a straight stitch, a zigzag and a patterned stitch.

Stitching with the feed dogs down

Free machine stitching is a great technique and used by many textile artists. As soon as you feel comfortable with free machining techniques on ordinary fabrics, then you are ready to get started with these new materials.
If you wish to be organised about your explorations, follow the exercises described below, if not, throw caution to the wind and just stitch into those metals!

Set your machine to free stitching by replacing the normal presser foot with a darning foot and set the machine to darning by dropping the feed dogs or covering them with a plate , whichever method your machine requires.

• Take a small patch of metal, place it onto a background fabric with stabiliser behind and stitch around the edge of the metal in a 'sketched line' motion, moving forwards and backwards in a direction parallel with the edge of the metal. Don't be shy about going over the end of the metal and into the fabric.

• Work around another patch of metal but stitching in a wavy line which moves between the metal and the background. Once you have attached the piece, continue working around the edges in a free, wobbly shape! I usually proceed either by stitching around the edge again in a wavy line three or four more times making sure that each time round I work into a different piece of the metal, or use a 'figure of eight' which moves forward slightly each time. These stitches disguise the edge of the metal where it meets the background especially if you use the same colour of thread as the background fabric. If worked on a fabric which has a pile such as velvet, the metal will appear to be growing outwards from the backing.

• Stitch freely across the surface of a piece of metal in any and all directions with a free straight stitch and on another piece with a free zigzag.

Combining surfaces

You will be able to stitch to any surface with any of the metals, meshes or knitted tubes, so experiment for yourself. Try using leather, suede, paper, felt, silk and fibre papers, cocoon strippings, Angelina® fabric, painted surfaces, knitted fabrics, reclaimed fabrics - the list can go on.
Don't forget that you can add metal to metal, metal to mesh, mesh to metal – not necessarily using a traditional fabric at all. I find that it is possible to stitch through up to four layers of 0.12 mm (0.004") annealed copper shim. When using the meshes, fine threads do shred more easily than when working on shim and if the mesh is crumpled, it is harder to stitch than even several layers of metal and does seem to break needles more often, so work more slowly.

Fine foils

The fine foils are very easy to stitch and simply can be treated as a thin fabric - no additional instructions being needed. The metal is sufficiently fine to allow the use of any thread that your machine likes to stitch with.
You can lay the foil flat or scrunch it, then place it onto a backing and stitch into it. Because they are so thin, foils will tend to break up under intense, dense stitching giving distressed, disintegrating surfaces. If you decide to prevent some of this disintegration you need to bond the foils into place first or add one or more layers of fine chiffons over the top.

Stitch exercises

Stitched ultrafine copper

Copper curls on velvet

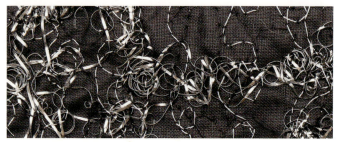

Pan scrubber!

'**Copper curls**' and pan-scrubbers can be a little more temperamental to stitch. Unless they are spread over a backing surface quite thinly, they do tend to break needles. It helps to place a layer of soluble film over them whilst stitching, also work steadily taking care as you approach denser areas of metal.

Machine stitched couching

A textured and patterned surface is obtained by stitching down thin twisted or plaited mesh strips.

Set your machine to a free machining zigzag (4 or 5 width) and stitch the mesh strips on in lines or patterns. You can also cut strips approx 20 mm (3/4") wide, fold along the length and crumple or pleat a little.

Using a straight free stitch follow the centre line of your mesh strip and stitch down in flowing waves or circles. The strips will need to be close together so that the edges of the strips are held up by the next strip.

... advise'd respects ...

A reminder...
Remember that after working with patinated metals you must clean your machine, bobbin case and bobbin area very well and keep your machine well oiled to prevent any rusting occurring in your machine.

Appliqué and reverse appliqué

You can of course choose to attach fabrics or other embroidered work onto the metal or mesh using any of the stitch methods we have covered. Indeed adding sections and shapes of layers of fabrics and meshes will add complexity, richness and interest to your work. A fun effect can be seen when stitching some of the looser metal meshes onto fabrics with a pile, as the pile peeks through the mesh from behind in intriguing ways. 'Reverse' or 'cut away' appliqué techniques create more understated, restrained surfaces. The metal will play a subtle, less prominent role as it is only seen in areas which you choose to expose.

To begin place layers of fabric on to a backing of metal or mesh and stitch over in a design which allows for areas to be cut thus revealing the different layers of fabric underneath right down to the metal.

Try placing sections of sheer manmade fabrics over a metal mesh with a final layer of sheer fabric covering the whole area, pin these into place and stitch over with a pattern (these can be drawn onto the back of the mesh and the first line stitched through from the back to make the process easier).

Between the areas of design either cut away with fine scissors or burn away with a fine heat tool such as a soldering iron or similar - not forgetting to work on a heatproof surface - revealing the underlying metal surface.

I think that this combination of layered sheer fabrics and the sheen of the metal mesh is a very successful mix.

Variations on this technique are to lay two or three full layers of sheer fabric over the mesh, stitch as before but then only cut away some areas of the sheers and fold back these flaps back securing them with a stitch or a bead; or to 'bubble' man-made sheer fabrics in either a flame or with a heat gun before laying them onto the mesh (pg. 47), stitching and finally burning away some of the fabric layers.

Metal and FibreDK (Lutradur®)

I am particularly fascinated by the use of materials or surface finishes which, when treated with another process, will react differently from each other to produce an interesting surface. To use materials such as FibreDK, or Tyvek® or Fibretex in conjunction with a metal or a metal mesh is always an intriguing option.

Try it for yourself by painting any heat reactive fibre. Stitch this down in areas or layers onto a material which is resistant to the effects of heat such as the metals we are using, then apply heat from a heat gun and see what happens!

Layers ready to go and stitched, folded piece

Copper mesh revealed from under layers of sheer fabrics

More revealing ...

Bubbled sheers in reverse appliqué

FibreDK layers over metal mesh and heated

Stitched and ready to dissolve

Stitched and ready to dissolve

Copper curls stitched in a sandwich of soluble films

... are vanishing, or vanished out of sight ...

Using soluble films as a stabiliser for stitch or to protect the bed of your machine from damage has already been mentioned, but we are able to be much more creative with soluble films than simply these practical measures. The possibilities for using metals and meshes placed onto a backing of soluble fabric which are then stitched through and together on the sewing machine create pieces which belie the perception of metals as being heavy and dense media to use.

As a starting point, shaped or manipulated sections of metal can be placed down onto soluble film and stitched into place using linking stitches added between the sections.
Once all sections are linked, continue to stitch or add hand stitching and other embellishments to your satisfaction, then place the piece in water and dissolve away the backing. For this technique, the only obvious caution to note is that you must ensure that all of the finishes on the metal or mesh, the threads and fabrics or other materials which you add to the piece are able to withstand immersion in water for as long as the backing takes to dissolve.

As to which of the many soluble media to use from those available, I tend to prefer the heaviest weight of water soluble film called 'Romeo', this allows me to work without an embroidery frame supporting the work and as it is clear, I can see where I am stitching if I build several layers of metal, mesh and stitch together or sandwich small pieces between two layers of soluble film.
However if you prefer to work with other forms then the principles are still the same.

Try to vary the size and shape of the metal pieces you attach in this way as effects from bold metallic surfaces with small gaps and holes between the sections to delicate lacy structures using small pieces of metals and meshes which build patterns and interesting connections can be developed.

step-by-step projects

... that with gentle work did frame ...

... on sea's rich gems ...
... strange shadows ...
... the glowing of such fire ...
... but makes antiquity ...

A selection of projects to try using techniques for working with metal shims and meshes

... on sea's rich gems ...

A pretty panel with embossed and painted metal in sea blues, handstitched, encrusted and surrounded with textured fabric and many faceted beads – a real gem from the sea!

... what need'st thou ...

Equipment you will need ...
Embossing tool
Soft embossing mat
Hard embossing mat
Plain general **scissors**
Usual **sewing requisites** including sewing scissors and needles

Materials you will need ...
36 gauge **aluminium** (or similar),
150 x 50 mm (6 x 2")
At least two colours of **nail varnish** or **glass paint**
A **stabilizing backing**
approx. 150 x 250 mm (6 x 10")
Your choice of **main fabric** of the same size as above
In the example a Habutai silk background and a silk paper with a little Angelina® added were used
A **sewing cotton** of a colour to tone with the background fabric and your bead selection
A pleasing selection of **beads** from your collection. Include a variety of surfaces such as matt, faceted, cut glass such as crystal, semi-precious chips, small sequins etc.
Metallic-silk tissue or other textured fabric,
approx. 150 mm sq.(6" sq.)

What to do ...

Copy the design given (Pic. 1) or draw a design of your own onto thin paper to a size of 50 x 150 mm (2 x 6"). I have designed a pattern of circles and waves reminiscent of the seaside.

Place your piece of aluminium onto the soft embossing mat and your pattern on to the top of this.
Draw over the pattern with the embossing tool. Remove the tracing paper and emboss into the pattern increasing the depth of the indents by working from both sides of the metal (Pic. 2).
Moving onto the hard mat, redefine some of the shapes by using the embossing tool around the raised designs as a last stage.

Paint the metal with nail varnish. I have used a mixture of blue, olive green and glitter varnishes. Allow to thoroughly dry then cut into three smaller pieces following around the lines of the design and cutting the edges into curved shapes (Pic. 3).

Pin a stabilizing fabric behind your main fabric and place the painted metal pieces in a vertical line along the centre line of the background fabric. Using sewing cotton hold the metal pieces into place by handstitching with a simple overstitch at intervals around each section.
It is easier to bring the needle up from behind just outside of the edge of the metal, and push down through the metal from the front (Pic. 4).

Cut your textured fabric into thin strips and stitching these horizontally between the metal areas, placing them in gentle waves to give a natural feel (Pic. 5).

Stitch your beads around the margins of the metal areas so that the edges are fully covered over and continue adding beads in a random, scattered way becoming more spread out as you move away from the metal areas (Pic. 6).

Your finished embroidery can then be presented stitched onto a canvas or book cover or mounted in a frame.

Pic. 2

Pic. 3

Pic.4

Pic. 5

Pic. 6

... advise'd respects ...

Taking these ideas further might include using other designs and layouts for the metal sections, use different colouring techniques and consider adding your favourite hand stitching.

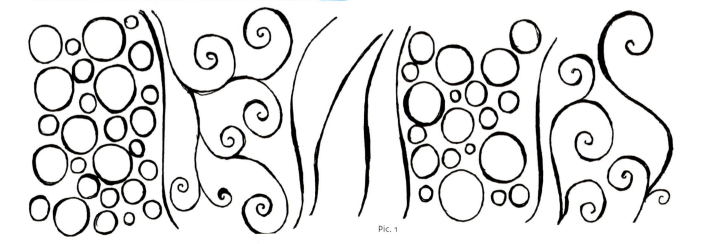

Pic. 1

... strange shadows ...

A deceptively delicate, layered hanging with a subtle balance of pewter and stainless steel meshes, printed and enamelled surface designs.

If you are not confident with free machine embroidery, this is especially designed for you as the stitching is completely achieved with the sewing machine feed dogs up for normal stitching.

In the piece shown here, I have used a flower design and a balance of surfaces which pleased me! Each of you, when making your panels, will find that your printing looks different to mine and your sense of pleasing proportions in a piece will also perhaps be different. These factors demand that you take a personal judgement and trust yourself to make decisions about the final balance of elements in your piece.

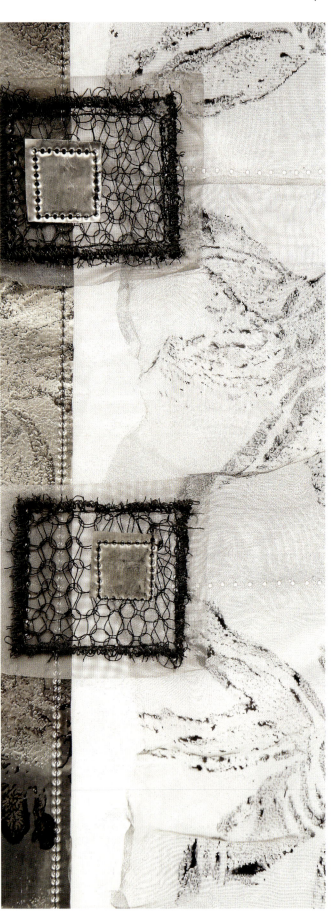

... what need'st thou ...

Equipment you will need ...

Paint roller

Acrylic plate or smooth plastic base for roller and paint

Pad of newspaper or similar as a **print pad**

Print blocks; pre-formed blocks include wooden print blocks, molding mats etc., or cut and score your own blocks from Pressprint, PZCut or similar

Craft heat gun

Tidy Tray

General but sharp **scissors**

Sewing pins

Sewing machine set for standard stitching

Materials you will need ...

Pewter or aluminium approx 300 x 150 mm (12 x 6")

Mediumweight stainless steel mesh
           approx. 300 x 300 mm (12 x 12")

Lightweight stainless steel mesh
           approx. 300 x 300 mm (12 x 12")

Coarse **knitted black wire** tube approx. 450 mm (18")

Acrylic paints in black and stainless steel or silver

Platinum or silver **embossing powder**

Charcoal coloured **sewing thread**

'Invisible' **Nylon sewing thread**

'Romeo' **soluble film** 450 x 500 mm (18 x 20")

Perspex rod between 10 mm (3/8") diameter
                              x 300 mm (12") long

What to do ...

Take about 1/4 of the lightweight mesh and the pewter metal, around 3/4 of the mediumweight mesh and all of the knitted wire tube from your original materials and place these on one side. These will be used during the collage and assembly process, balancing the patterned areas that you are about to create.

Decide on the pattern(s) that you are going to use for printing. You might have a preformed print block you like or make your own personalised print blocks using Pressprint or similar.
Here I have blocks based on a flower pattern in four different sizes (Pic. 1 overleaf and pic. 2).

Prepare your area and materials for printing. Squeeze out some black and stainless steel acrylic paint onto a flat plastic surface and load the roller (Pic. 3). Do not over-load the roller or your printing will be 'sludgy'! Roller straight across about 1/3 of each of your materials. Leave these to dry (Pic. 4).

... advise'd respects ...

Because we are printing onto mesh, some paint will penetrate through the mesh onto the print pad underneath each time. Therefore take care that you change the top surface of the print pad between prints to prevent any carry over of paint.

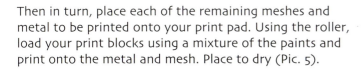

Then in turn, place each of the remaining meshes and metal to be printed onto your print pad. Using the roller, load your print blocks using a mixture of the paints and print onto the metal and mesh. Place to dry (Pic. 5).

Prepare a working area for using embossing powders. You will still need the print pad and also the heat gun, the tidy tray and the embossing powder.
Take a selection of printed and unprinted pieces of your metal and mesh and the print block(s) of your choice. Load the block(s) with ink from your stamp pad and transfer this to the metal and mesh (Pic. 6). Whilst the ink is still wet, place the metal or mesh pieces over the tidy tray, sprinkle the embossing powders over and shake off, finally heat to fix (Pic. 7) (see pg. 19). On a larger piece of metal you might want to do this in several stages as it makes the process easier to handle.
Your metal materials are now all ready to use.

To begin assembling the piece you will need to cut some of the metal and meshes into smaller sections.
Arrange these sections into a pleasing balance by looking for areas of denser colour to balance lighter or plainer areas. Some places in the design can have a 'busy' feel with several overlaid surfaces and tightly spaced elements whilst others should give a breathing space and be clear from clutter.

I have concentrated on simple rectangles and squares and arranged the design as a series of interlocking elements. You could follow this idea or develop a pattern which suits your pieces.

Pic. 2

Pic. 3

Pic. 4

Pic. 5

Pic. 6

Pic. 7

Pic. 8

It may take a while to decide on your final design, but when you are happy with the layout you are ready to assemble the piece.

Allow 50 mm (2") at the top edge to make a tube for slotting the Perspex rod into.

To stitch your elements together, consider the options as follows:

The **type of thread** for each section – is it the grey or the invisible thread?

The **type of stitch** – is it to be a straight or a zigzag stitch?

The **length and width of your stitching**.

By keeping a sensitive balance of these simple options the stitching will become a part of the design not simply a means of attachment.

Begin by placing the piece which is furthest to the back onto your soluble film and pin into place. Then pin one or two other areas into place over this and stitch into place using your machine.

Continue placing the elements of your piece onto the soluble film background and stitching.

When all of your elements are stitched, fold the top of the piece away from you and make a sleeve wide enough for your Perspex rod with a straight stitch.

When you have completed all of the stitching and trimmed away the loose threads, you are ready to dissolve away the soluble film. Place the entire panel into hand hot water, laying it as flat as possible and leave for at least twenty minutes, changing the water after the first five minutes. Take your piece out of the water and when you can no longer feel any sticky residue, allow it to dry.

Slot the rod into its tube and your piece is ready to hang (Pic. 8).

... advise'd respects ...

Once you have tried this, other options for development which you could consider are using different mixes of materials, heat burnishing or other paint effects, adding other materials or other types of stitching.

If you use only metals and meshes and only nylon thread then your piece should be suitable to be displayed outside. If you have used materials which will patinate over time in the outdoors, your piece will continue to develop and integrate into the environment.

Pic. 1

... the glowing of such fire ...

This dramatic panel catches the changes of light, shimmering and reflecting with a fiery glow.
This is very characteristic of my use of metals, relying for its impact on the bright, smooth burnished copper juxtaposing the textured, matt threads of the stitching.
Burnished copper allows a wide range of thread colour schemes to be used, you could explore these or vary the metal or mesh type. Taking the ideas further would involve developing different patterns or adding further stitching or embellishing on the surface.

... what need'st thou ...

Equipment you will need ...
Sewing machine set to free stitching with a darning foot

Materials you will need ...
Heat burnished copper,
approx. 250 x 400mm (10 x 16")
'Romeo' **soluble film** 300 x 450mm (12 x 18")
Red, orange and maroon **sewing threads**
Red orange and maroon (or similar) **thicker threads** for use in the bobbin of your sewing machine
10 mm **MDF** board cut to 200 x 350mm (8 x 14")
Acrylic paints in yellow, gold, red and purple.
Paint brush
Strong **adhesive** such as a contact adhesive
Polyurethane or acrylic **spray varnish**
One picture hanging **D-ring**

Pic.1

Pic. 2

Pic. 3

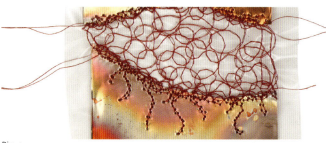

Pic. 4

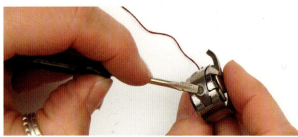

Pic. 5

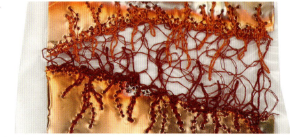

Pic. 6

What to do ...

Paint the MDF board with a mixture of the colours. Try to paint with a stippling type of action and mix the colours into swathes of colour across the surface with no hard edges between the colours.

Make sure that you paint all the front and sides plus a border of approx. 25 mm (1") around the edge at the back. Leave this to dry (Pic. 1).

Take the heat-burnished copper and cut it into strips along the width. Make sure that the strips each have wavy edges and are different in size. Also ensure that the first and last strips, which will have a straight edge from the top and bottom of the metal piece are at least 75 mm (3") deep at their narrowest as these will wrap around the back of the MDF panel. You will not be using all of the original metal because you are leaving open gaps to stitch across on the project so save these leftovers for another project.

Mark a rectangle 250mm x 400mm (10 x 16") with a biro pen onto the soluble film and arrange your metal sections into the marked area. Consider the order of colours which you will be using in your stitched areas.

I have chosen to use the orange thread at either end of the piece, moving through red to maroon in the centre. You can follow this or choose a different arrangement of colours.

Mark your colour areas on the soluble film in biro (Pic. 2).

Now stitch the metal into place with a wavy line of stitch, moving between the metal and the soluble backing. Remember to change your thread to suit the colour marked onto your soluble film (Pic. 3).

When all of the pieces are held in place, use the appropriate colours of thread to stitch circles all over each of the gaps in the soluble film, making sure that these stitched circles interlink with each other and with the edge of the metal sections. You can also stitch further into the metal sections with wavy lines or swirls or circles. Once you are happy that your pieces are all linked by stitch, trim away all of the loose thread ends (Pic. 4).

Now add the thicker threads by using 'cable stitch' (one of my favourites!). To work with this stitch you will need to loosen the tension screw on your bobbin case by approximately 1/2 a turn and fill bobbin cases with each of the colours of your thicker threads in turn (Pic. 5).

Once the machine is threaded with your thicker thread in the bobbin and a normal sewing thread of matching colour in the top, place the panel under the machine with the right side down and away from you and begin to add the stitching. Aim to create a line of small circles along the boundary edge of the metal and the soluble fabric and then continue to work in extended patterns or lines to compliment your previous stitching. Repeat this across each boundary of metal and soluble, changing the thread colour to integrate with the colour scheme (Pic. 6).

When you have completed all of the stitching and trimmed away the loose threads, you are ready to dissolve away the soluble fabric. Place the entire panel into hand hot water, laying it as flat as possible and leave for at least twenty minutes, changing the water after the first five minutes. Take out of the water and once you can no longer feel any sticky residue, allow it to dry.

Spread the adhesive over the back of the metal and press the painted side of the MDF into place over the top. Turn it over and check that the pieces are spread out on the board as you wish and the metal pressed flat to the board, then neatly fold all of the edges around to the back and leave the glue to set. You will find that the making process has introduced some crinkles into the metal - this will simply add to the reflective qualities of the finished piece. Cover the raw metal edges on the back with a strong tape and add a picture mounting D-ring approx. 2/3 of the way up the back in the centre and you are finished! (Pic. 7)

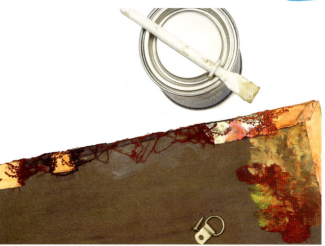

... advise'd respects ...

When cable stitching I use the bobbin filler on the sewing machine to give an even tension on the thread and I test the stitching on a spare piece of fabric. You are aiming to get a smooth line of thicker thread along the underside of the fabric looking like a hand couched line. If the bobbin tension is too tight it will drag and tend to jam in the machine, if too loose it will make a knobbly loose line and also tend to jam!

Pic. 7

Spice bags are characteristic of Indian nomadic tribes and form a decorative bag equally practical as an evening bag.
I have mine hung with lavender in the living room.
The simplicity of construction gives scope for a highly decorated surface and the use of a woven metal mesh gives the bag a wonderful structural feel whilst still being translucent.

... what need'st thou ...

Equipment you will need ...
Sewing machine set for free machining and with a darning foot
Nightlight candle
Water pot
Medium **embossing pad**
Embossing tool

Materials you will need ...
Burnished **stainless steel mediumweight mesh**, 300 mm (12" sq.)
Nylon organza in one or more colours (I have used a plumy-purple organza), approx. 500 mm (20")
Machine **embroidery thread** to match the organza
Metallic sewing thread in gold or copper
Metallic hand stitching thread in a similar colour to the metallic sewing thread
Cord or ribbon for the straps, approx. 2 m (80")
(I have twisted a mixture of hand stitching threads and a metallic thread to create a cord)
Approx. 400 x 3mm flat **sequins** in metallic blue
Approx. 350 x **4mm gold or copper beads** (I have used beads with a gold lining and a matt 'AB' finish)
Approx. 600 x small (approx. size 11) **gold or copper rocaille beads**

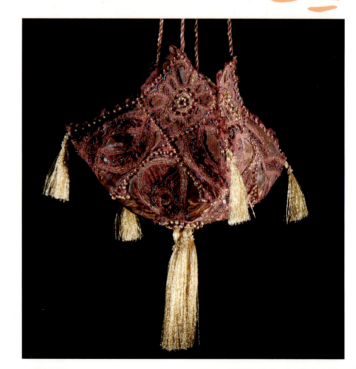

What to do …

Place the burnished (pg. 12) stainless steel mesh over a medium embossing pad and mark out the pattern as shown in Pic. 1 with a biro or embossing tool (Pic. 2). (You could take the easy way out and enlarge the design on a photocopier!)

Cut the nylon organza into sections between approximately 100 x 300 mm (4 x 12") and 300 x 300 mm (12 x 12"). Hold each section of fabric in turn over a lit nightlight candle. Do not pull too tightly. Allow the material to begin to shrink and bubble (Pic. 3), moving the fabric over the flame until the whole of each piece becomes textured.

… be of thyself so wary …

Always do this in a well ventilated area with a face mask on. Always work with a pot of water nearby which is large enough to plunge both the piece you are working on and your fingers into in case of an accident.

Now lay the pieces of organza fabric over the whole area of stainless steel mesh and allow them to overlay each other. Ideally you will have sufficient fabric to place at least two layers over the whole piece of stainless steel mesh. Pin these into place making sure that the embossed pattern line which you have drawn is on the rear of the piece so that you can still see it (Pic. 4).

Using a toning coloured thread, stitch a single machine line from the back of the mesh to outline the entire pattern using free machine stitching (Pic. 5).

Turn your piece to the front again and continue to stitch around the pattern making strong lines to identify the pattern as seen in Pic. 6.

Pic. 2

Pic. 3

Pic. 4

Pic. 5

Pic. 6

Pic. 1

Pic. 7

Pic. 8

Pic. 9

Pic. 10

You are now ready to leave the sewing machine and begin to embellish by hand. Using a metallic machine thread, hand stitch in small crosses between the lines of the pattern and then add beads add sequins in ordered patterns over the piece. (Pic. 7 and 8)

Make four small tassels approx 50mm (2") long and five larger ones, approx. 100mm (4") long, adding small beads around the top of the tassel to add interest. The four small tassels should to be stitched at the centre point of each edge of the square and the five larger ones around the centre circle.

To form the bag shape, fold the project in half. From the fold join 2/3rd's of the length with a close running stitch on each side. Now take the middle point of the unstitched sides and pull out into a fold. Once again stitch from this fold to 2/3rd's of the length of each side.

Cut your cord (or ribbon) into two equal lengths and stitch one end of the first cord to the inside of a pointed corner and the other end of this cord to the opposite corner. Repeat this for the other two corners with the second piece of cord (Pic. 10).

... what beauty is, see where it lies ...

ann small
val hunt
jeanette kilner
alysn midgelow-marsden

Metals have been used widely as a textile material or by artists who become fascinated by their properties.
The following are a selection of inspiring artists.

ann small

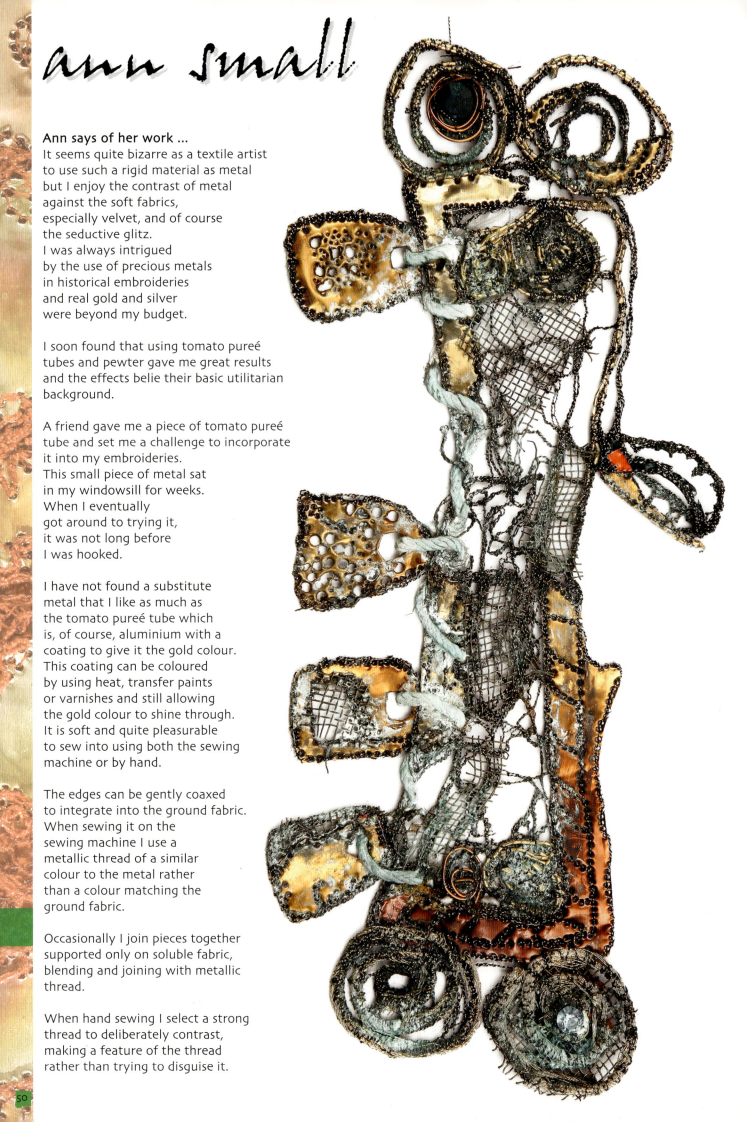

Ann says of her work ...

It seems quite bizarre as a textile artist to use such a rigid material as metal but I enjoy the contrast of metal against the soft fabrics, especially velvet, and of course the seductive glitz. I was always intrigued by the use of precious metals in historical embroideries and real gold and silver were beyond my budget.

I soon found that using tomato pureé tubes and pewter gave me great results and the effects belie their basic utilitarian background.

A friend gave me a piece of tomato pureé tube and set me a challenge to incorporate it into my embroideries. This small piece of metal sat in my windowsill for weeks. When I eventually got around to trying it, it was not long before I was hooked.

I have not found a substitute metal that I like as much as the tomato pureé tube which is, of course, aluminium with a coating to give it the gold colour. This coating can be coloured by using heat, transfer paints or varnishes and still allowing the gold colour to shine through. It is soft and quite pleasurable to sew into using both the sewing machine or by hand.

The edges can be gently coaxed to integrate into the ground fabric. When sewing it on the sewing machine I use a metallic thread of a similar colour to the metal rather than a colour matching the ground fabric.

Occasionally I join pieces together supported only on soluble fabric, blending and joining with metallic thread.

When hand sewing I select a strong thread to deliberately contrast, making a feature of the thread rather than trying to disguise it.

For me metal works best in small units which are joined with either stitch or fabric allowing the embroidery to flex.
It is tempting to over use it and for a time I plastered in onto everything. Now I am a little more selective and save it for small precious adornments and making mounts for gems.

Pewter which is rather expensive has the effect of melting into the fabric and careful blending can give the appearance of molten silver poured on the fabric.
I also enjoy its weight.
Fabric heavily applied with pewter looks and feels very expensive.

val hunt

Val says of her work ...

I use a diverse selection of rubbish in my work, but my favourite material is drinks can metal. This obsession began several years ago after drinking the contents of a can, then experimenting with the can. I found that the metal could be formed and constructed and because I love textiles, I am constantly experimenting to find new ways of constructing and forming the metal to give it textile qualities.

Through using and experimenting greatly with drinks cans over the years I now understand the character, qualities and limitations of this material. I use this pliable, light material in much the same way that a textile artist uses fabric. I cut, weave, pleat and frill a material which is essentially flat and two dimensional to make a three dimensional form. Intricate patterns can be imprinted on the surface and the can's graphics also add interesting character and history.

I find inspiration from natural forms, surface textures, strata formation, layers, lines, form, construction, texture and the exciting diversity of textiles. Also found slipping into my work are animals, birds, historical fashion, Egyptian and tribal art and not forgetting the humorous side of life which is also important and is conveyed in many of my works.

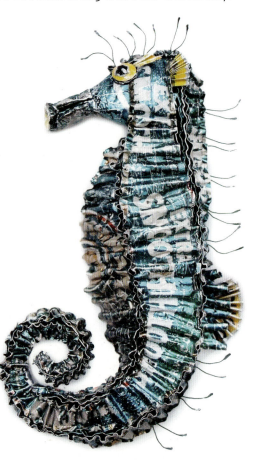

My love of creative experimentation with recycled material is a constant adventure into the unknown. Because one is working with unconventional material in an unconventional way, with unconventional tools, the end results can be very exciting, rewarding and often unexpected. Coming from a family of inventors, I love the challenge of solving the numerous practical problems which arise when creating something. My work is always changing as I experiment with and discover new techniques.

Even as a child, I remember gaining tremendous satisfaction from recycling a discarded object in a creative way.

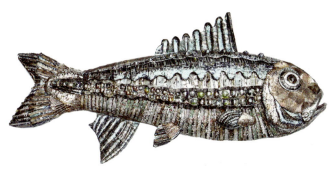

I believe that there is great hidden potential for creativity and scope for inventiveness from using 'throw away material'. The ecological, economical and accessible reasons are all equally important to me. Great satisfaction is had from sitting in my workshop with a large box of rubbish on one side and creditable craft items on the other!

Fortunately getting the raw material is no problem as family and friends are very happy to leave bags of empty cans and rubbish outside my door.

My work ranges from small jewellery pieces which are amazingly light, user friendly and easy to wear, through to large sculptures and wall pieces.

jeanette kilner

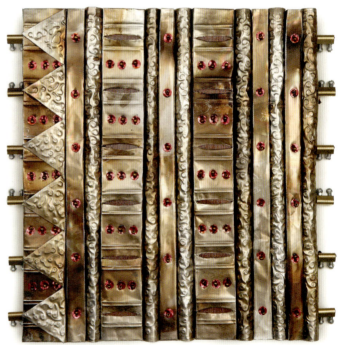

Jeanette says of her work ...

The main challenge of using aluminium cans is their limited size. If used untreated, the metal will snap if it is folded and unfolded too many times, so after cutting the can open and flattening the usable section, I anneal them using a blow-torch. This does two things, firstly it makes the metal softer and more pliable and secondly it changes the colour from silver to shades of gold. Occasionally, depending on the can's lining the colours can be almost iridescent. I like the unpredictability of how the cans change colour, as this often suggests ways in which they can be used.

I create constructed panels from aluminium cans using designs based loosely on sections from historic costumes – a 'Fortuny' pleated dress, a slashed Elizabethan sleeve, the pin-tucked yoke of a Victorian nightdress, or the padded hem of an 1820's brocade dress.

I have deliberately exploited my understanding of the visual qualities of different textile techniques to experiment with translating these qualities into other materials, including metal.

The aim is to simulate the surface textures and patterns found in fabrics without necessarily using the textile techniques themselves.

The cans can be embossed to give the effect of brocade, embroidery stitches, and woven textures by moulding over dowel, or cutting and folding to form tabs, pleats, tucks etc. Extra pieces of metal can be added by literally stitching them with wire, including coloured areas from untreated cans. I also add glass or metal beads, coloured copper wires, mother-of-pearl buttons, and metal meshes when necessary.

I originally started working with cans because I enjoy the challenge of working with re-cycled and found materials, making something special out of waste, and also because I like being able to produce work using the minimum of specialist equipment.

alysn

I use metal shim and metal meshes in place of fabric, altering the original metal by burnishing, texturing and patterning. These combine with stitch to create subtle combinations explored through dense repeating and interlocking pattern based designs of squares, triangles, zigzags, spirals and radials that have been used by people throughout the history of mankind.

As you observe the pieces, the patterns emerge slowly resulting in warm harmonies through subtly gentle, yet obsessive mazes. At once disconcerting and fascinating.

This series is comprised of a range of evocative forms and figures incorporated into surfaces which are articulated with complex, undulating, knotted and interwoven designs and text, declaring a personal narrative.

midgelow-marsden

Derived from personal markings such as fingerprints and body markings, my designs aim to evoke the working of our unconscious human ancestral memory. Further through the pixelization of images, I create a mosaic of forms and patterns which appear to move and change, swaying in the tides of unseen forces.

These pieces, when seen together, hint at the connections and flows of energy around one particular life which are interpreted in phrases and sayings, text and narrative stitched into the works and explicitly linked to each of the pieces. I aim to achieve a happy invention of form and daring conceptualization, conspiring to combine a composition of lines and geometric patterns with a narrative which considers the spark of creativity and its' constraints in real life.

it takes time to see

Having read this book and hopefully been inspired to try a selection of ideas, I urge you to continue to play and sample techniques. Once started you will realise the myriad variations in materials, scale, additions, designs and end results by using these novel materials with their unique properties.

Do not feel restricted by the use of an unusual material, think of this as an adventure and an opportunity to create pieces in a very different way. Taking a moment to consider the scale at which you work will reap great rewards. Creating very small works for jewellery or hair pieces; larger for book covers and wall panels; or the opposite extreme, think about very large hangings or art quilts.

Consider the attraction of the manipulations and changes which we have addressed with the metals , then add to this other media, fabrics and surfaces which are already in your personal repertoire.

The sheen and reflectivity of metal juxtaposing the richness of a plush velvet, or worked, aged and antiqued metallic surfaces added to a leather or treated papers, the smooth resistant surface of metal versus a pliant or web-like fabric or mesh of threads ....

... I could go on, but it is for you to find your path and explore the possibilites.

... many a thing I sought ...